The Greenwoods SOLVE One-Step Equations

Brandy Crump

Illustrations by RKS Illustrations

Copyright © 2018 by Brandy Crump

All rights Reserved. This book may not be reproduced in whole or in part without the expressed written consent from the publisher, except by reviewer who may quote brief passages in a review. Nor may any part of this book be reproduced, stored in a retrieval system, or transmitted in any form or by any means, recording, photocopying, mechanical, electronic, or without the written permission of the publisher.

ISBN: 978-1-7335296-5-5

[ ] + − × ÷ = ? ( )

This book is dedicated to my baby that I miscarried in 2009. It was the pain of losing you that birthed this book series.

To my children, Myles and Bria, who inspire me to leave a legacy.

To Mr. Brown, former math teacher and coworker of 10 years, who kept asking me every single day, "Did you finish your books yet?" Well, Mr. Brown, I can finally say "YES!"

To Chris Nolen, former math teacher of 20 years and CEO of Nferno Productions, who read my manuscripts and said, "Hurry up and put those books out there!"

To the students who struggle in math and require simple explanations with examples of how it connects to their daily lives.

[ ] + − × ÷ = ? ( )

[ ] + − × ÷ = ? ( )

"Just 30 minutes left. Soon, class will end and Spring Break will begin!" thought Miles. He has been looking forward to this day for months. His family is going to the Tranquility Beach Resort for Spring Break. "It is going to be perfect," thought

[ ] + − × ÷ = ? ( )

[ ] + − × ÷ = ? ( )

Miles. "Mom will relax at the spa while dad plays golf. Brea and I will have nonstop excitement as we ride roller coasters, play video games, and swim in the resort's amusement park."

[ ] + − × ÷ = ? ( )

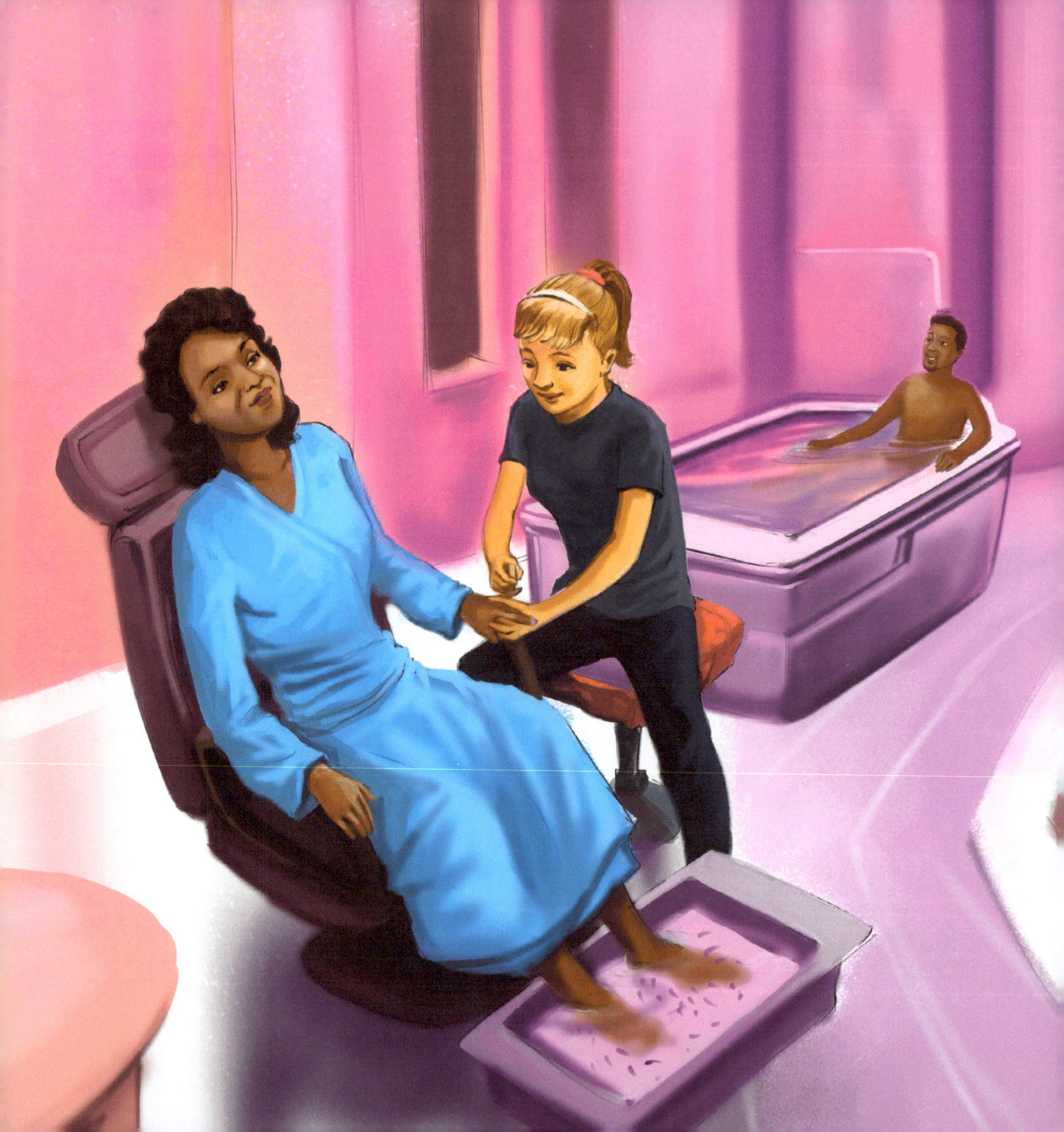

Mr. Nolene, Miles' seventh-grade math teacher was at the board teaching a lesson on solving one-step equations. Mr. Nolene displayed the following chart on the board:

The Key to Solving Equations

Given Operation	The Operation Needed to Solve
Addition $x + 1 = 4$	Subtraction Solve by subtracting 1 from both sides $x + 1 = 4$ $-1 = -1$ $x = 3$

Subtraction x − 1 = 4	Addition Solve by adding 1 to both sides $$\begin{aligned} x - 1 &= 4 \\ +1 &= +1 \\ x &= 5 \end{aligned}$$
Multiplication 2x = 8	Division Solve by dividing both sides by 2 $$\begin{aligned} 2x &= 8 \\ \frac{2x}{2} &= \frac{8}{2} \\ x &= 4 \end{aligned}$$
Division $\frac{x}{2} = 3$	Multiplication Solve by multiplying both sides by 2 $$\begin{aligned} (2)\frac{x}{2} &= 3(2) \\ x &= 6 \end{aligned}$$

Fraction in front of a variable? $\frac{1}{2}x = 5$	Multiply by the reciprocal to get rid of the fraction
	The reciprocal of $\frac{1}{2}$ is $\frac{2}{1}$, so multiply both sides by $\frac{2}{1}$ $\frac{1}{2}x = 5$

$$\frac{(2)}{1}\frac{(1)}{2}x = 5\frac{(2)}{1}$$

$$1x = \frac{(5)}{1}\frac{(2)}{1}$$

$$x = 10$$

After Mr. Nolene discussed the chart, he called various students to the board to demonstrate more examples. The first student to go to the board was Miles because Mr. Nolene could tell that Miles' mind was elsewhere and he didn't want Miles' grade to drop. Miles' problem was to solve $x + 2 = 5$. As requested, Miles went to the board and wrote the following:

$$x + 2 = 5$$
$$-2 = -2$$
$$x = 3$$

Mr. Nolene told Miles that he was correct. He erased the problem and then wrote

$$x - 2 = 7$$

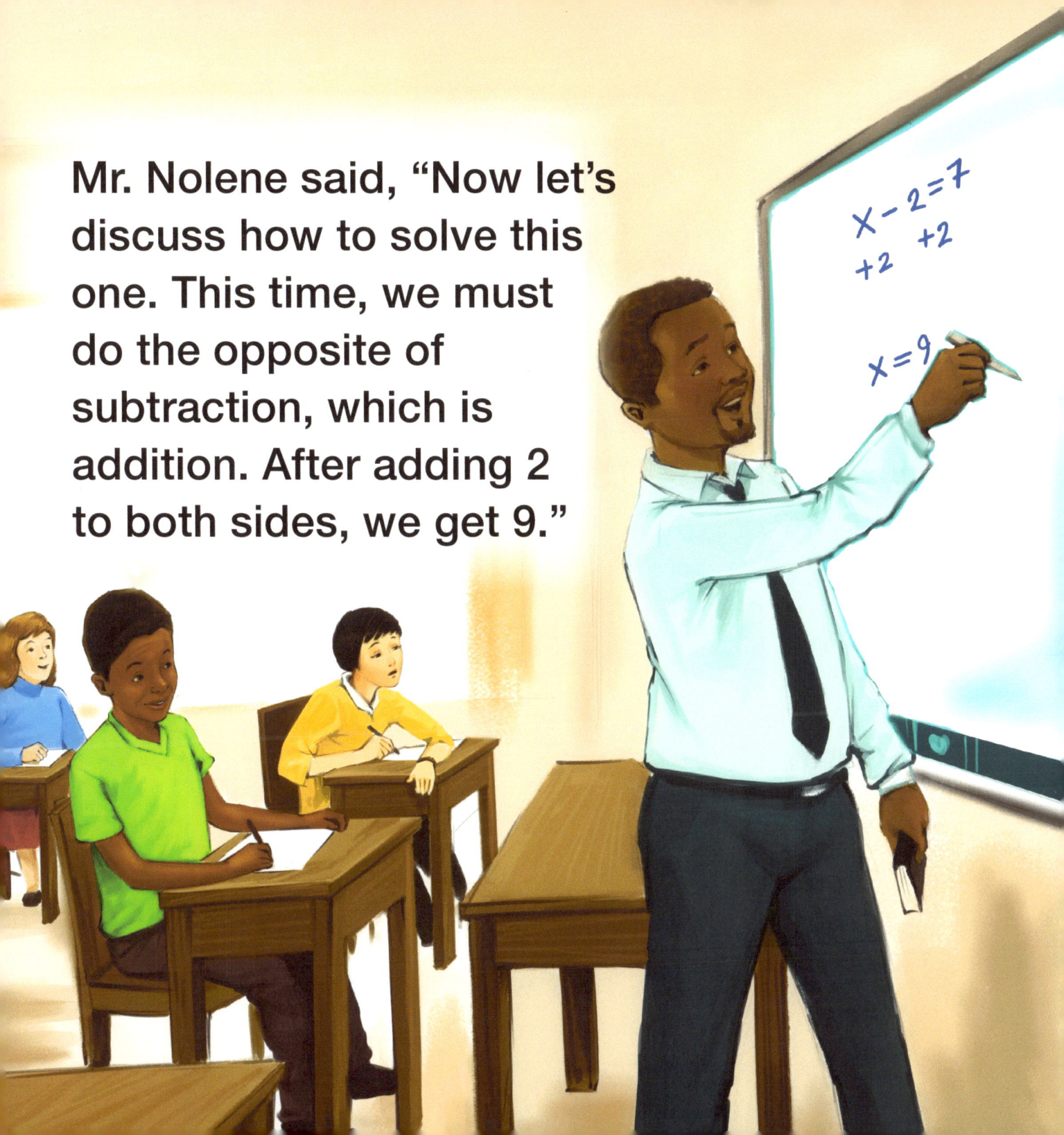

Mr. Nolene said, "Now let's discuss how to solve this one. This time, we must do the opposite of subtraction, which is addition. After adding 2 to both sides, we get 9."

$x - 2 = 7$
$+2 \quad +2$

$x = 9$

"Now students, I want you to create your own problems. Let example 3 be multiplication and 4 be division. Solve both problems and explain how to solve them with a brief statement. I will come around to check your progress."

Miles wrote the following:

Example 3
$2x = 10$
$x = 5$ (I divided both sides by 2 and got 5)

Example 4

$$\frac{x}{4} = 12$$

x = 48 (I multiplied both sides by 4 and got 48)

Mr. Nolene checked all of his students' papers and then said, "I am pleased to say that everyone understands how to solve one-step equations. Therefore, I expect to receive great work from you on this Spring Break Project." Immediately, Mr. Nolene

[ ] + − × ÷ = ? ( )

began distributing the project. Just as the students began complaining, Mr. Nolene interrupted and said, "No sense in complaining because this counts as a test grade and is due upon your return from Spring Break." Mr. Nolene proceeded to read the directions to the class. "You must create 4 equations to represent real-life situations. You must have 1 addition, 1 subtraction, 1 multiplication, and 1 division problem to get full credit. Have fun, and, most importantly, be safe while on break. Class is dismissed."

[ ] + − × ÷ = ? ( )

Miles walked at a fast pace to meet his little sister, Brea, at her classroom and then they boarded the school bus together. Miles began looking out the front window of the bus as if it would make the bus move faster. After about an hour of dropping off other students, Brea finally looked out the window to gain her bearings. "Look Miles, there's the Longer-Life Gym, which means our stop is the next one," said Brea. Suddenly the bus came to a stop. It was as if the bus was listening to Brea and following her command. As soon as they stepped off the bus, they saw Mom waving her hand; she was signaling for them to cross the street. Usually, Miles and Brea walk home from the bus stop, but today they are going on vacation and their parents plan to beat the rush-hour traffic.

"How was school?" Mom asked. "It was hard to focus because all I could think about was going on vacation," replied Miles. "Well, I had fun," said Brea. "My teacher gave us a pizza party because we had the most students on honor roll this quarter. We had treats and even watched a movie!" Brea exclaimed. "Well, you definitely had a ball but did she give you some homework?" inquired Mom. "Yes mam, she gave us a math worksheet and a book to read. We must write a book report," replied Brea. "Now that really sounds like fun," Dad said sarcastically. "What about you, Miles?" asked Mom. "My math teacher, Mr. Nolene, gave us a math project where we must use equations to represent real-life situations," replied Miles. "I don't know why he gave us this hard assignment when he could have given us a simple worksheet like all the other teachers," complained Miles. "Well, I think it's great that he gives challenging work with real-world application," replied Dad. "Well, I'm going to need some help with this," said Miles. "No problem, you will see the importance of this assignment by the end of our vacation," Dad said.

After driving for about an hour, Brea started her usual line of questioning. "Are we there

[ ] + − × ÷ = ? ( )

yet?" "No beautiful, we still have about 2 hours to go," replied Dad. "Brea, you are a genius!" Dad said excitedly. "What did I do, Daddy?" asked Brea. "You just gave me an idea for our first equation. Miles, write this down: 80 miles + x miles = 175 miles. This equation represents the number of miles we have driven plus how many we have left before we reach our destination," said Dad. "Now Miles, you need to solve the equation to find how many more miles we need to drive," said Dad.

[ ] + − × ÷ = ? ( )

[ ] + − × ÷ = ? ( )

$$80 + x = 175$$
$$-80 = -80$$
$$ x = 95 \text{ miles}$$

Since 80 was positive, Miles subtracted it from both sides of the equation to get 95 miles.

Once the family arrived at the resort, they ate dinner and then went bowling. These two events led to the development of Miles' next equation. Dad paid $120 for dinner and another $100 on bowling. When the

[ ] + − × ÷ = ? ( )

Greenwood family returned to their room, Dad only had $50 left. Miles wrote the following equation to calculate the amount of money Dad had prior to dinner and bowling:

$$x - 120 \text{ (dinner)} - 100 \text{ (bowling)} = 50 \text{ (left over)}$$
$$x - 220 = 50$$
$$+ 220 = +220$$
$$x = \$270$$

Miles added 220 to both sides of the equation because the opposite of negative

220 is a positive 220, and 220 + 50 equals $270.

The next day, Mom gave the kids $30 to spend at the game room. Miles and Brea spent the entire $30 purchasing 100 tokens. "Miles, I bet we can play 1000 games with all these tokens," Brea said excitedly. "Brea, you just gave me an idea for another equation. I can write the equation $4x = 100$ to represent the number of games we can play since each game requires 4 tokens and we have a total of 100 tokens," Miles said.

"Well, it looks like we can afford to play only 25 games, Brea," said Miles.

After leaving the game room, the Greenwood family went to dinner. Miles saw this as an opportunity to discuss the final problem for his math project. "Dad, I still need one more problem and it must] be an equation that includes division," said Miles. Mom and Dad looked at each other

[ ] + − × ÷ = ? ( )

and began to laugh uncontrollably. In fact, Mom laughed so hard that tears started rolling down her face. Miles and Brea were confused because they didn't hear nor see anything funny. Finally, Dad stopped laughing and disclosed his and Mom's inside joke. "Son, all we do is divide! Mom and I divide our money with you and your sister all the time," said Dad.

[ ] + − × ÷ = ? ( )

[ ] + − × ÷ = ? ( )

"For instance, let's say I have x dollars to spend on tonight's dinner and this amount must be split between the four of us. This can be represented with

$$\frac{x}{4} = ?$$

Now, let's set the equation equal to 30 because we will spend $30 on each person. Thus, the equation becomes

[ ] + − × ÷ = ? ( )

[ ] + − × ÷ = ? ( )

$$\frac{x}{4} = 30$$

To solve for x, you multiply both sides by 4 to get x = 120. Therefore, the amount we have to spend on dinner is $120."

The Greenwood family ate dinner and then spent their last night of the vacation watching a movie outside in the resort's park.

[ ] + − × ÷ = ? ( )

Brandy Crump is the author of a math book series which includes the following titles: (1) The Greenwoods Add and Subtract Fractions with Like Denominators, (2) The Greenwoods Add and Subtract Fractions with Unlike Denominators, (3) The Greenwoods Multiply and Divide Fractions, (4) The Greenwoods Simplify Percents, (5) The Greenwoods Add and Subtract Integers, (6) The Greenwoods Solve One-Step Equations, and (7) The Greenwoods Solve Proportions. Brandy holds a bachelor's degree in Secondary Math Education and a master's degree in Educational Administration. She has 18 years of experience in teaching mathematics to at-risk students who suffer from adverse childhood experiences (ACES). She grew up in Harvey, Illinois, and graduated from Thornton Township High School where she taught for 14 years. As the product of an underserved, poverty-stricken, and high-crime community, she experienced ACES that prepared her to better understand and connect with her delinquent and at-risk students. She has provided workshops on effective classroom management through mutually respectful relationships and increasing student engagement through cooperative groups and authentic learning activities. Brandy is a lifelong learner and continues to research best practices for reaching out to struggling students. She is a member of Delta Sigma Theta Sorority Incorporated. She enjoys working with the youth in her community, writing books, creating math games, and conducting motivational speaking engagements.

www.ingramcontent.com/pod-product-compliance
Lightning Source LLC
LaVergne TN
LVHW072058070426
835508LV00002B/164